Contents

The Old World
CONNECTION

A continent is a huge **landmass** on the surface of the Earth. We generally speak of seven continents: Europe, Asia, Africa, North America, South America, Australia and Antarctica. Some continents are completely surrounded by water, such as Australia and Antarctica. Other continents are physically connected or attached to one another, such as North America and South America.

The three continents most closely connected to one another are Europe, Asia and Africa. These are known as 'Old World' continents. Some people speak of Australia as one of the Old World continents, even though it is not physically connected to Europe, Asia or Africa. This is because Australia lies in the world's Eastern Hemisphere, the half of the Earth that is shared with these other three continents.

Human events

The name 'Old World' is somewhat misleading. Europe, Asia and Africa are not really older than the other continents. They are called 'Old World' because some of the oldest events in human history took place on these continents. For example, scientists believe that the first humans developed in Africa and then spread throughout Asia and Europe. Most of the earliest civilisations, with ancient towns and cities, also appeared on these continents. And it was from the Old World continents that people set out to explore and settle other lands of the Earth, such as the Pacific Islands, Australia and the Americas. Many people living in these newer settlements today have Old World ancestors and still speak a language and follow customs that come from Europe or Asia.

Europe, Asia and Africa are known as the Old World continents.

Close links

There is a very large area of land where the different Old World continents join together. Europe and Asia have the largest of these areas (they are attached for thousands of kilometres between the Ural Mountains and the Black Sea). Two large countries, Turkey and Russia, have territory in both continents. In areas where the continents connect, they have many things in common.

The climate, plants and animals around the connecting regions are often the same. People around these regions often share the same language or religion – even though they belong to different countries or continents. For example, millions of people who live in the Middle East – the region where Asia and Africa come together – speak the Arabic language and follow the religion of **Islam**.

Eurasia or Eurafrasia?

There is no clear, definite boundary between Europe and Asia. In fact, most **geographers** say that Europe and Asia are not really two separate continents, but part of one larger continent called Eurasia. Some geographers would go further and say that Africa is not a separate continent either, since it is connected to Asia around the Sinai Peninsula, where Egypt and Israel come together. Geographers who group Europe, Asia and Africa together call this great continent Eurafrasia.

The Parthenon in the Greek city of Athens was built more than 2000 years ago. People have lived in Athens for more than 5000 years.

Introducing
EUROPE

The name 'Europe' comes from the old Middle Eastern word Erub, meaning 'land of the setting sun'. In size, Europe is one of the smallest continents (only Australia is smaller). Yet Europe has the third-largest population of all the continents.

As we know, Europe is not a true continent, but a continuation of the Eurasian **landmass**. Why, then, is Europe called a continent? The reason is cultural more than anything else. Most of the early geography books were written by Europeans. They believed their land was the most important in the world, and that it must be distinguished from non-European lands, such as Asia and Africa. This was a narrow view. Even so, Europe does have a powerful influence over the rest of the world. European ideas (such as democracy and communism) and European languages (such as English, French and Spanish) have spread throughout the world, influencing the history of all other continents and their countries.

In size, Europe is one of the smallest continents.

ICELAND
Reykjavik

NORWAY
SWEDEN
FINLAND
RUSSIA

Atlantic
Ocean

Helsinki
Oslo
Stockholm
ESTONIA
Moscow

UNITED
KINGDOM
North
Sea
LATVIA
LITHUANIA

DENMARK
BELARUS

London
NETH.
Berlin
Warsaw
POLAND
UKRAINE

BELGIUM
GERMANY
LUX.
CZECH REP.
SLOV.
MOLDAVIA

Paris
AUSTRIA
HUNGARY
ROMANIA

FRANCE
SWITZ.
CROATIA
Bucharest

BOSNIA
HERZ.
SERBIA
BULGARIA

PORTUGAL
ITALY
MACEDONIA

Madrid
Rome
ALBANIA

SPAIN
GREECE
Athens

Mediterranean Sea

N
W   E
S

0   1000 km
0   600 miles

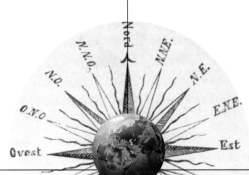

EUROPE, ASIA & AFRICA
Old World Continents

Continents

Bruce McClish

www.heinemann.co.uk/library
Visit our website to find out more information about Heinemann Library books.

To order:
☎ Phone 44 (0) 1865 888066
▤ Send a fax to 44 (0) 1865 314091
▢ Visit the Heinemann Bookshop at www.heinemann.co.uk/library to browse our catalogue and order online.

First published 2003 in Australia by Heinemann Library a division of Harcourt Education Australia, 18–22 Salmon Street, Port Melbourne Victoria 3207 Australia (a division of Reed International Books Australia Pty Ltd, ABN 70 001 002 357).

Editor: Carmel Heron
Designer: Stella Vassiliou
Photo researcher: Margaret Maher
Production controller: Chris Roberts
Maps and diagrams by Pat Kermode and Stella Vassiliou

Film separations by Digital Imaging Group (DIG), Melbourne, Australia
Printed in China by WKT Company Ltd.

ISBN 1 74070 127 5 (hardback)
07 06 05 04 03
10 9 8 7 6 5 4 3 2 1

ISBN 0 431 18162 4 (paperback)
09 08 07 06 05
10 9 8 7 6 5 4 3 2 1

British Library Cataloguing in Publication Data
McClish, Bruce
Europe, Asia & Africa: old world continents - (All About Continents)
910'.021811
A full catalogue record for this book is available from the British Library.

Acknowledgements
The author would like to thank: Avi Olshina, geologist, Victorian Government; Peter Nunan, geography teacher, Royal Geographical Society of Queensland; Craig Campbell, researcher; Jenny McClish, researcher and contributing author.

Main cover image of African scene supplied by PhotoDisc.

Other images supplied by: AFP/AAP/M. L. Carapezza: p. 8; Auscape/Jean-Paul Ferrero: p. 11; Australian Picture Library (APL): pp. 19, 29; APL/Corbis/© Tiziana and Gianni Baldizzone: p. 23, /© David Cumming: p. 21 (bottom right), /© Owen Franken: p. 24, /© Gail Mooney: p. 9, /© Robert van der Hilst: p. 13 (left), /© Patrick Ward: p. 25; PhotoDisc: pp. 5, 7, 10, 13 (right), 15, 17, 21 (top left & right, bottom left), 27.

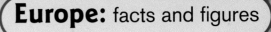

Europe: facts and figures

Europe has **mineral wealth**, rich farming soils, big cities and millions of skilled, educated workers. This makes Europe a world leader in farming, business and industry.

Area: 10 450 000 sq km	
Climate: mainly **temperate**, with large areas of forest, woodland and grassland	
Population: 701 188 000 (estimated 2002)	
Biggest country: Russia (area of European Russia 3 955 800 sq km)	
Highest peak: Mt Elbrus (5642 metres above sea level)	
Lowest point: Volga Delta (28 metres below sea level)	
Largest freshwater lake: Lake Ladoga (18 400 sq km)	
Longest river: Volga River (3688 km)	
Crop products: wheat, oats, barley, rye, potatoes, sugar beets, grapes, wine, olive oil, sunflower seeds	
Animals and animal products: cattle, sheep, pigs, poultry, dairy products, fish	
Mineral products: petroleum, natural gas, coal, iron ore, zinc, nickel, manganese, bauxite, lead, potash, uranium	
Manufactured products: automobiles, steel, machinery, chemicals, clothing and textiles	

Europeans enjoy a high **standard of living**.

Landforms

Europe has a great variety of landforms for such a small continent – including mountains, plains, rivers, lakes, coasts and islands. Many European countries have all of these features.

Mountain ranges

Europe's highest peaks are in the Alpine Mountain chain. The famous Swiss Alps, with the pyramid-peaked Matterhorn, are part of this chain. The Alpine Mountains are made up of several ranges in southern Europe, including the Pyrenees, Apennines, Balkans and Caucasus Mountains. The slopes and valleys of these ranges are often covered with magnificent forests and **fertile** farmland.

The oldest mountains in Europe are in the north-west corner of the continent, in places such as Sweden, Norway and Scotland. These mountains are much more worn-down than the Alpine Mountains. The climate is cold and the land is poor for farming, often covered with rocks or bogs.

Mt Etna, on the Italian island of Sicily, is the largest active volcano in Europe.

Plains

The best farmlands of Europe are in the plains that stretch from France to Russia. These plains are made up of level land, as well as rolling hills. Some of the plains were shaped by glaciers (masses of moving ice) that covered much of Europe during the **Ice Age**, many thousands of years ago. Today, the plains have some of the most fertile farmlands in the world. The densest (most closely packed together) populations, the biggest cities and the busiest industries are located on the European plains.

Rivers

Rivers are very common in Europe. Since ancient times, Europeans have used rivers for many purposes – fishing, docking boats, transporting goods and making pirate raids. Today, these rivers are still heavily used for transport and industry. The Volga and the Danube are Europe's longest rivers, while the Rhine is one of the busiest rivers. A European river can pass through several different countries, ports and cities throughout its course. Many European rivers have been lengthened or joined by canals to aid transport. There are so many canals in Europe that it is possible to cross the continent by boat.

Coast and islands

Only a few places in Europe are far from the sea. Europe has an extremely uneven coastline, forming many bays and **peninsulas**. This makes the coastline very long – nearly 61 000 kilometres – more than double the length of Africa's coastline. Thousands of islands lie off the European coast. Some of these islands are large enough to hold entire countries, such as Ireland, Great Britain and Malta.

Diary of a continent

▶ **300 million years ago**
Swampy forests cover much of the continent (the remains turned to coal deposits).

▶ **200 million years ago**
Europe is part of a giant supercontinent called Laurasia (also made up of Asia and North America).

▶ **170 million years ago**
Much of Europe is flooded by shallow seas.

▶ **90 million years ago**
Europe breaks away from North America.

▶ **1 million–500 000 years ago**
Early humans enter Europe during the Ice Age.

Europe has many of the world's deepest caves, especially in France and Spain. Some of these caves go down more than a thousand metres.

Climate, plants and animals

A mild climate

Europe has some very cold lands near the Arctic Circle and some very dry lands near the Asian deserts. But most of Europe has a **temperate** climate, with mild weather throughout much of the year. The main cause of this mild weather is the sea. Warm ocean currents keep most of Europe's Atlantic coast free of ice during the winter, even in places such as Norway. Warm ocean winds bring plenty of rain to the land, feeding the rivers and carrying moisture throughout most of the continent. Yet there is also plenty of sunshine. The sunshine and moisture are good for crops, resulting in Europe's rich farmlands.

The sunniest area of Europe lies in the south. This includes parts of Spain, France, Italy, Greece and other countries bordering the Mediterranean Sea. These areas are well known for their long, hot, dry summers and cool, mild winters. In fact, any place in the world that has a similar climate (including certain parts of South Africa, Chile and California) is said to have a Mediterranean climate.

Most of Europe has a temperate climate, with mild weather throughout much of the year.

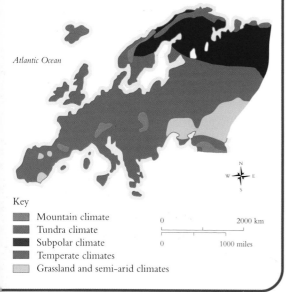

Atlantic Ocean

Key
- Mountain climate
- Tundra climate
- Subpolar climate
- Temperate climates
- Grassland and semi-arid climates

0   2000 km

0   1000 miles

Trees and forests

Although the European climate is good for trees, huge areas of forest have been cleared away over the past 2000 years. The largest remaining forests lie in the north of the continent. Two of the most common kinds of trees in Europe are the evergreen **conifers** (including fir, pine and spruce) and the broad-leaved **deciduous trees** (including beech, elm and oak). These are similar to the trees of North Asia and North America.

Olive trees grow best in Europe's sunny Mediterranean climate.

European animals

Wild animals of Europe are also similar to those of North Asia and North America. Typical examples include bears, wolves, foxes, elk, rabbits, squirrels, owls, sparrows and pigeons. A large number of wild animals have been wiped out, or greatly reduced in number. This occurred in the early days of European settlement, as a result of hunters killing the animals and farmers clearing the animals' **habitats**. Many remaining wild animals live in specially protected parks and reserves. Some kinds of animals that were once wild – including sheep, oxen, ponies and reindeer – are now **domesticated**.

Forests
- brown bear
- wolf
- red fox
- weasel
- wolverine
- lynx
- wild cat
- European polecat
- red deer
- roe deer
- wild boar
- beaver
- badger
- hedgehog
- shrew
- mole
- chipmunk
- red squirrel
- owl
- hawk
- common toad

Mountains
- ibex
- chamois
- alpine marmot
- asp viper

Mediterranean scrub
- rabbit
- wild sheep (mouflon)
- fallow deer
- Barbary ape
- scrubland partridge
- Mediterranean mole-rat
- whip snake

Grasslands
- marbled polecat
- saiga antelope
- marmot
- brown hare
- common vole
- European suslik
- black grouse

Polar regions
- polar bear
- wolf
- seal
- walrus
- reindeer (domestic)
- Arctic hare
- lemming
- ermine

Barbary apes are found on the tiny area of Gibraltar, a British territory south of Spain. The Barbary ape is the only wild monkey living in Europe.

History and culture

EUROPE

European culture has always been changing throughout history – sometimes slowly and sometimes quickly. Civilisation on the continent began about 5000 years ago.

Greeks and Romans

The powerful Greek and Roman civilisations influenced huge parts of Europe, Asia and Africa. They did this through trading and conquest. They also **colonised** many areas, establishing their language and customs in distant lands. The Greeks and Romans developed important ideas about art, mathematics, medicine, morals and law.

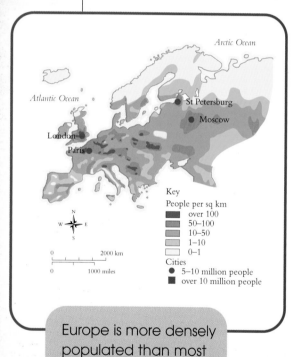

Europe is more densely populated than most other continents.

The Middle Ages

After the Roman **Empire** broke up around AD 400, the Middle Ages began. This period began in turmoil, as fierce tribes overran much of Europe, including the Huns, Vandals and Goths. These tribes came from outside the Roman Empire, and helped destroy it. The tribes later adopted **Christianity**, which became the main religion on the continent. The Catholic Church grew more powerful than any tribe or kingdom. Other important Christian groups – including the Anglicans, Lutherans and Methodists – developed later from the Catholic Church.

World powers

Between 1300 and 1600 came a period called the Renaissance, in which there was tremendous growth in art, science and exploration. By the 1800s, Europeans had the strongest, most efficient business and industry in the world, and had settled every other continent except Antarctica. Disaster struck in the 1900s, with two devastating wars. Millions of Europeans died in World War I and World War II, and large areas of city, town and farmland were destroyed. Yet Europe rapidly recovered from the destruction. Today, it is a world leader in many areas, including manufacturing, banking, farming and tourism.

Modern Europe

Most European countries are not very large in size, but they are heavily populated. Europeans are normally loyal to their country, but they are often just as loyal to their local area, city or town. Many people want to live close to their parents, brothers, sisters, grown-up children, grandparents and other relatives. This is especially true in southern Europe, where traditions of home and family are strongest.

Europeans are extremely proud of their history. They are eager to preserve their old buildings, monuments and works of art. This does not mean that all Europeans are old-fashioned in the way that they live. Often, a modern structure, such as a supermarket or a skyscraper, will stand near a cathedral or an ancient statue.

Facts about living in **Europe**

- About 50 languages are spoken in Europe. In many countries, different languages are spoken in different communities.
- Roman Catholics are the largest group of Christians in Europe today. Eastern Orthodox and Protestant groups are also numerous. Other European religions include **Judaism** and **Islam**.
- Europeans have some of the best health and education systems in the world. They enjoy a great variety of sporting and leisure activities – including tennis, football, cycling, skiing, swimming, hiking, sightseeing and going to restaurants and theatres.

Europe has some of the largest and most famous cities in the world, such as Moscow, Paris and London.

Although Christianity began in Asia, it developed into a major world religion in Europe.

Introducing
ASIA

The name 'Asia' comes from *Asu*, an old Middle Eastern word that means 'land of the rising sun'. Asia is the largest continent, with almost a third of the world's land area. It is also the most populated continent, with more than half the world's people and more than 40 countries. The world's most populated countries (China and India) are in Asia.

Asia contains the world's highest point (Mt Everest) and a very low point (the Dead Sea). It has some of the longest rivers, wettest forests, largest deserts and widest plains. Asia has not only a vast mainland, but thousands of islands, including those making up the countries of Sri Lanka, Indonesia, Japan and the Philippines.

> Asia is the world's largest and most populated continent.

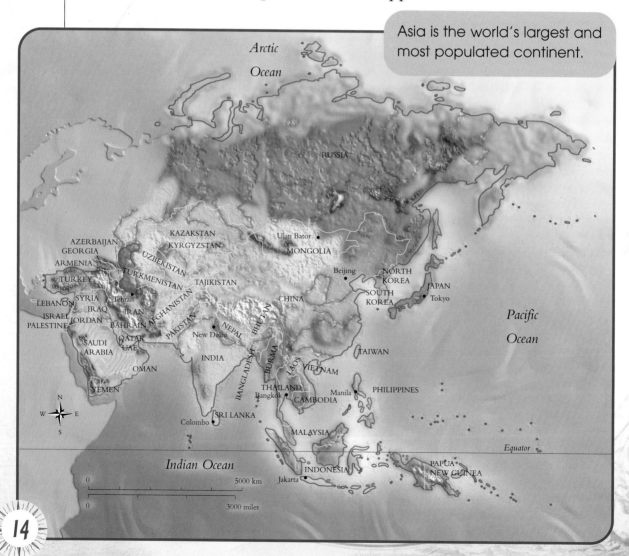

Although Asia is huge, much of the continent is too dry, too cold or too isolated for people to farm the land. Many people in Asia suffer from the problems of poverty and natural disasters, such as storms and floods. There is also conflict between different countries and cultural groups, such as Indians and Pakistanis or Arabs and Israelis.

A country road in India.

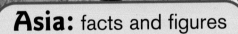

Asia: facts and figures

Area: 44 000 000 sq km

Climate: mainly temperate or tropical, with large areas of forest, grassland and desert

Population: 3 799 971 000 (estimated 2002)

Biggest country: Russia (area in Asia: 13 119 600 sq km)

Highest peak: Mt Everest (8850 metres above sea level)

Lowest point: the Dead Sea shore (400 metres below sea level)

Largest freshwater lake: Lake Baikal (31 500 sq km)

Longest river: Chang (Yangtze) River (6300 km)

Biggest desert: Arabian Desert (2 230 000 sq km)

Crop products: rice, wheat, rubber, cotton, silk, jute, soybeans, citrus fruit, spices, coffee, tea, sugar cane, palm oil

Animals and animal products: camels, goats, sheep, horses, pigs, yaks, reindeer, fish

Mineral products: petroleum, natural gas, coal, tungsten, tin, antimony, manganese, mica, chromite, iron ore, zinc, nickel

Manufactured products: steel, automobiles, ships, heavy machinery, electronic equipment, handicrafts, clothing and textiles

Lands and land regions

Asia is so big that it is commonly divided into several different land regions. Each one of these regions has its own distinct landscapes.

- The Middle East includes the countries of Saudi Arabia, Israel, Palestine, Iraq, Turkey and Iran. This is mainly a thinly populated desert region, with a scarcity of good farmland.

- South Asia lies in the region of India, Pakistan and Nepal. This is a highly populated region with many low, fertile plains and high mountain peaks.

- South-East Asia includes Thailand, Vietnam, Malaysia and Indonesia. This is a warm, rainy region, with large forest areas and many islands.

- East Asia is made up of Japan, North Korea, South Korea, Taiwan and most of China. East Asia is a highly populated region with a variety of landscape areas, including mountains, fertile plains, forest and grassland.

- Central Asia is a huge region that includes Mongolia, Tajikistan, Turkmenistan and western China. This is a land of deserts, high mountains and open, treeless plains. The region is mainly dry, with few areas that are good for farming.

- North Asia is the largest region on the continent. North Asia is the Russian land of Siberia, a thinly populated region of great forests, barren plains and long, harsh winters.

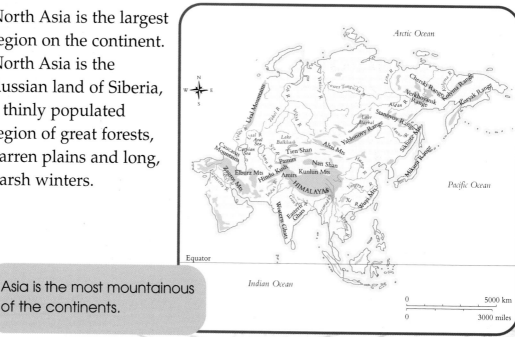

Asia is the most mountainous of the continents.

Mountains

Of all the continents, Asia has the most mountains. The highest mountains are in the Himalayas, with high, sharp peaks rising more than 8000 metres. Another high range is the Pamirs, which is known as 'the roof of the world'. The Altai Mountains are a lower, older range with very ancient rocks. Other important ranges include the Hindu Kush, Tien Shan (or Tian Shan), Karakoram and Zagros ranges. Many of these ranges form natural barriers, which have made it difficult for people of different countries and cultural groups to contact each other.

Deserts

A region of vast deserts stretches through the Asian continent, from Saudi Arabia in the west to China in the east. These deserts are not always hot; some can be very cold at times.

Rivers

Some of the most crowded areas of Asia are near rivers. River areas contain precious water and fertile soil. Away from the rivers, Asian landscapes are often barren, with much desert or rocky ground, and people have difficulty growing food. Important rivers of Asia include the Tigris, Euphrates, Indus, Ganges, Brahmaputra, Irrawaddy, Mekong, Chang (Yangtze), Hwang Ho, Lena, Ob and Yenisey.

Diary of a continent

► **200 million years ago**
Asia is part of the Laurasian supercontinent, along with Europe and North America.

► **90 million years ago**
Laurasia breaks up.

► **40 million years ago**
Himalayas begin to lift, as India collides with Asian continent.

► **2–1 million years ago**
Early humans enter Asia from Africa.

► **30 000–10 000 years ago**
Land bridge forms across Bering Strait, allowing humans to spread from Asia into North America.

► **10 000–5000 years ago**
First civilisations develop in Asia.

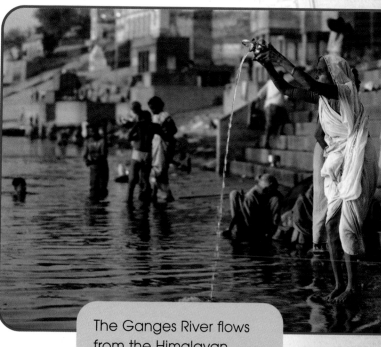

The Ganges River flows from the Himalayan mountains to Bangladesh.

Climate, plants and animals

Asian climates

Asian climates are extremely varied. This variety is caused by the huge size of the continent, reaching far into different climate zones. For example, parts of the dry Middle East may get no rain for years, while parts of tropical South Asia and South-East Asia have more than 3000 millimetres of rain every year.

Temperatures can also go to extremes. Most of South-East Asia is warm throughout the year, while parts of North Asia are always frozen. Generally, the tropical areas of South Asia and South-East Asia are warm and wet, while more northern and central areas of the continent are cooler and drier, especially in the desert and high mountains. The Middle East is mainly hot and dry.

Monsoons

A monsoon is a strong wind that blows over South Asia, South-East Asia and neighbouring regions. Monsoons change direction with the season. During the winter, monsoons blow from the inland region. These winds are cool and dry, and bring drought to many areas. During the summer, monsoons blow from the warm tropical seas. These winds carry heavy rain clouds over the land. Many Asian farmers depend on summer monsoons for rain, though they often bring disastrous storms and floods.

Plants

Just as the climates of Asia are extremely varied, so are the plants. In the deserts of the Middle East there is often little or no vegetation. Central Asia is well known for dry, open grasslands, called steppes. In the wetter parts of South Asia and South-East Asia, plants grow abundantly, producing valuable resources, including nutmeg, rubber, bamboo and tea. North Asia has huge forests of conifers, although only small vegetation grows on the frozen tundra regions.

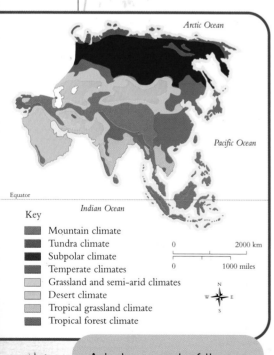

Arctic Ocean

Pacific Ocean

Equator

Indian Ocean

Key
- Mountain climate
- Tundra climate
- Subpolar climate
- Temperate climates
- Grassland and semi-arid climates
- Desert climate
- Tropical grassland climate
- Tropical forest climate

| 0 | | 2000 km |
| 0 | | 1000 miles |

N
W E
S

Asia has most of the different climate regions.

Wildlife

Asia has many animals that are similar to those of nearby continents. Asia has elk, reindeer, wild sheep, bears, foxes and hares similar to those of Europe and North America. It also has camels, elephants, antelopes, monkeys, apes and crocodiles similar to those of Africa. Yet Asia has some unique animals, such as the panda and komodo dragon, which are found nowhere else in the world. Asia also has a surprising variety of cats. These include tigers, leopards and lynxes, as well as some unique kinds, such as the snow leopard and the fishing cat. The continent's greatest variety of animals is found in South Asia and South-East Asia.

Domestic animals

Many areas of Asia are now too crowded by people for wild animals to live there. Nevertheless, domestic animals are still common, even in the most crowded areas. Some of the most common domestic animals were first tamed in Asia, including cattle, horses, sheep, pigs and chickens. Camels, elephants, yaks and water buffalo have also been **domesticated** in Asia. These larger animals are used for heavy work, as well as for food and sources of hides or fur.

Temperate forests and mountains

- brown bear
- wolf
- red fox
- wolverine
- lynx
- snow leopard
- giant panda
- yak
- ibex
- red deer
- sika deer
- beaver
- pika

Tropical forests

- tiger
- leopard
- fishing cat
- monkey
- orang-utan
- gibbon
- giant flying squirrel
- Malayan tapir
- Asian elephant
- rhinoceros
- water buffalo
- flying frog
- python

Grasslands

- mongoose
- marbled polecat
- saiga antelope
- marmot
- brown hare
- common vole
- hamster
- pangolin
- cobra

Deserts

- sand fox
- Bactrian camel
- wild ass
- Arabian oryx
- tortoise
- desert locust

Polar regions

- polar bear
- wolf
- Arctic fox
- walrus
- reindeer
- Arctic hare
- lemming

The komodo dragon is the world's largest lizard.

History and culture

The earliest civilisations began in Asia. They began more than 5000 years ago, before the first European civilisations. Asians were the first to develop farms, cities, the wheel, the plough, law, writing and even paper. All the world's major religions – **Hinduism, Buddhism, Judaism, Christianity** and **Islam** – came from Asia.

Powerful kingdoms

Some of the earliest Asian civilisations were the Sumerian of the Middle East, the Indus of South Asia and the Shang dynasty of China. Although these civilisations eventually ended, they were replaced by other important Asian kingdoms and empires. Some of them, such as the Persians, Huns, Mongols, Arabs and Ottomans, were powerful enough to conquer large parts of Europe and Africa. However, by the 1800s and 1900s, most of these kingdoms were weakened. European countries had invaded, colonised and taken over many Asian regions. Some Asian countries had to fight wars to free themselves of a foreign invader; others were given their freedom peacefully. Although Asian countries are independent today, many of the people still dress in a European manner or speak a European language.

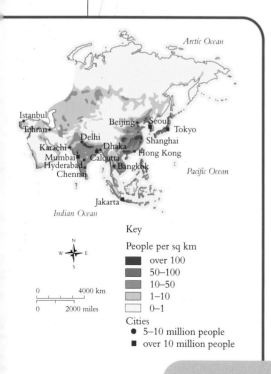

Arctic Ocean

Istanbul
Tehran
Karachi
Mumbai
Hyderabad
Chennai
Delhi
Dhaka
Calcutta
Beijing
Shanghai
Hong Kong
Bangkok
Seoul
Tokyo

Jakarta

Indian Ocean

Pacific Ocean

Key

N W E S

0 — 4000 km
0 — 2000 miles

People per sq km
- over 100
- 50–100
- 10–50
- 1–10
- 0–1

Cities
- ● 5–10 million people
- ■ over 10 million people

People and culture

Despite such amazing variety in regions and cultures, most Asians have certain things in common. For example, the family is extremely important. Asians are often expected to obey their parents – not only as children, but also as adults. Besides family, most Asians have close ties to some other group, such as a clan, social class or religious body. Members of each group are not always friendly with the members of different groups, even those in the same country or living nearby. Sometimes there are violent clashes between different groups, such as Jews and Muslims or Muslims and Hindus.

Although Asia holds more people than any other continent, there are large areas where practically no one lives.

Traditional lifestyles

Growing crops or raising animals is the most typical occupation in Asia. Many Asians lead a very traditional lifestyle, one that is not so different from the lifestyle of their ancestors. This is especially true for groups of **nomadic** people, who roam from place to place, never staying in one permanent location. These people get most of their food and clothing from herds of sheep, goats, camels or yaks. Nomadic people still roam throughout many regions of the continent, such as the Middle East and Central Asia.

Facts about living in **Asia**

- Most people live in mountain valleys, along rivers or near the sea.
- More people follow Hinduism than any other Asian religion. Most Hindus live in India. Islam, also widely followed, is the most widespread religion on the continent. Few areas of Asia do not have large groups of Muslims (followers of Islam). Another common religion is Buddhism, especially in South-East Asia.
- Hundreds of different languages are spoken in Asia. Many Asian countries have more than one language group.
- More people speak Mandarin Chinese than any other language in the world.
- Poverty is widespread in Asia.

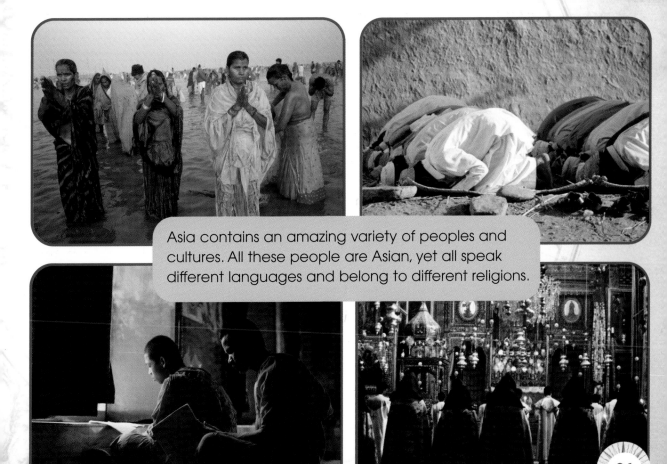

Asia contains an amazing variety of peoples and cultures. All these people are Asian, yet all speak different languages and belong to different religions.

Introducing
AFRICA

Africa is the second-largest continent. It is larger than the combined areas of Europe, Australia and India. Africa has the world's largest desert (the Sahara) and the world's longest river (the Nile). It also has the biggest land animal (the African elephant) and the fastest land animal (the cheetah).

> Africa is the second-largest continent in size and population.

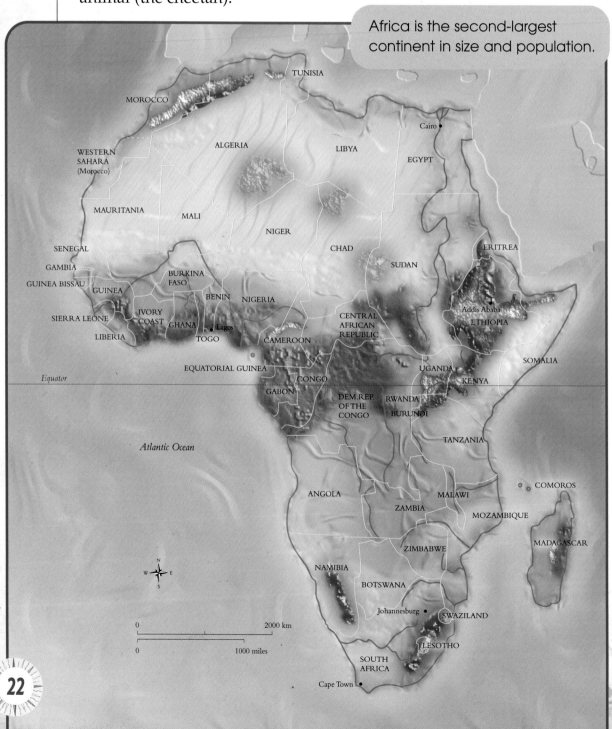

TUNISIA
MOROCCO
Cairo
WESTERN SAHARA (Morocco)
ALGERIA
LIBYA
EGYPT
MAURITANIA
MALI
NIGER
SENEGAL
CHAD
ERITREA
GAMBIA
SUDAN
GUINEA BISSAU
BURKINA FASO
GUINEA
BENIN
NIGERIA
Addis Ababa
ETHIOPIA
SIERRA LEONE
IVORY COAST
GHANA
Lagos
CENTRAL AFRICAN REPUBLIC
LIBERIA
TOGO
CAMEROON
EQUATORIAL GUINEA
UGANDA
SOMALIA
Equator
CONGO
KENYA
GABON
DEM. REP. OF THE CONGO
RWANDA
BURUNDI
Atlantic Ocean
TANZANIA
COMOROS
ANGOLA
MALAWI
ZAMBIA
MOZAMBIQUE
MADAGASCAR
ZIMBABWE
N
W   E
S
NAMIBIA
BOTSWANA
Johannesburg
SWAZILAND
0   2000 km
0   1000 miles
LESOTHO
SOUTH AFRICA
Cape Town

The name 'Africa' probably comes from the old Roman word *aprica*, which means 'sunny'. Africa is indeed a continent of blazing sunshine, with huge areas of hot desert and tropical grassland. It is also a continent of great civilisations and ancient cultures. Today, Africa is made up of more than 50 independent countries. More people live in Africa than any other continent, except Asia. Even so, most areas in Africa are thinly populated.

Africa is a continent of wealthy resources, especially in minerals, farms and forests. Yet most of the African people are poor. Many people are also troubled by war, famine, drought and disease.

Africa: facts and figures

Area: 30 300 000 sq km

Climate: mainly tropical, with large areas of grassland, desert and rainforest

Population: 831 437 000 (estimated 2002)

Biggest country: Sudan (2 505 810 sq km)

Highest peak: Mt Kilimanjaro (5895 metres above sea level)

Lowest point: Lake Assal in Djibouti (155 metres below sea level)

Longest river: Nile River (6670 km)

Biggest freshwater lake: Victoria Lake (69 485 sq km)

Biggest desert: Sahara (9 100 000 sq km)

Crop products: coffee, bananas, cocoa beans, cashews, yams, cloves, vanilla beans, palm kernels, **cassava**, rubber, coffee, cotton, corn, millet, peanuts, rice, **sorghum**, sugar

Animals and animal products: camels, goats, cattle, sheep, anchovies, mackerel, sardines, tuna, fish oil

Mineral products: gold, petroleum, cobalt, vanadium, chromite, manganese, platinum, copper, diamonds, phosphate, uranium, iron ore, natural gas, antimony, tin

Nomadic Woodabes with cattle, Niger. Drought and spreading deserts are a major problem in Africa.

Landscapes

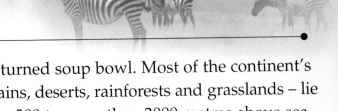

Africa is somewhat like an upturned soup bowl. Most of the continent's landscapes – including mountains, deserts, rainforests and grasslands – lie on a high tableland, or plateau, 300 to more than 2000 metres above sea level. The plateau drops sharply near the coastline, where there is a narrow rim of low-lying farmlands, beaches and swamps.

The Sahara Desert is larger than the continent of Australia. The Sahara is mostly made up of gravel, boulders and sand dunes. Some of its regions are mountainous.

Mountains

Africa's mountains are scattered throughout the high plateau. The Atlas Mountains of North Africa form the continent's longest range, stretching 2400 kilometres. The Atlas Mountains lie close to Europe, and often resemble the Alpine Mountains, with snowy peaks and slopes densely forested with oak and pine.

The highest mountains in Africa are old volcanoes, such as Mt Kilimanjaro. Although this mountain lies in the hot tropical region, its peak is always covered with snow and ice (the name Kilimanjaro means 'the mountain that glitters'). Other mountains include Mt Kenya, Mt Cameroon, the Ruwenzori Range, Drakensberg Range and the Ethiopian Highlands. There are also some high mountains in the Sahara Desert.

Rivers and rapids

The Nile is the most important river in North Africa. It flows through the Sahara Desert, creating one of the few moist, **fertile** areas in this generally **barren** region. For thousands of years, the Nile Valley has been one of the few densely populated regions on the continent. Cairo, also located on the Nile, is Africa's largest city. Rivers in other parts of Africa include the Limpopo, Zambezi, Congo, Orange and Niger. Since most of Africa's rivers flow down from a high plateau, they often have places with rapids and waterfalls. This can make it dangerous to travel by boat or raft, but it does offer magnificent scenery. Victoria Falls on the Zambezi River is one of Africa's most popular tourist attractions.

Valleys and lakes

The Great Rift Valley in East Africa is a rugged volcanic region of fertile soil and deep valleys. Some of these valleys hold Africa's largest lakes, including the massive Lake Victoria. Although not as large, nearby Lake Tanganyika is the longest freshwater lake in the world (680 kilometres in length). Rivers and lakes of Africa are an important source of fish for people who live far from the sea.

Diary of a continent

▶ **550 million years ago**
North Africa lies over the South Pole.

▶ **250 million years ago**
Southern Africa is covered with glaciers in a great **ice age**.

▶ **200 million years ago**
Africa is part of the Gondwana supercontinent, along with Antarctica, Australia, India and South America.

▶ **150 million years ago**
Gondwana breaks up; Africa drifts away.

▶ **20 million years ago**
The Great Rift Valley begins to form.

▶ **5 million years ago**
African climate becomes drier, with grasslands replacing many forest areas.

▶ **2 million years ago**
First humans develop in southern and East Africa.

The turbulent waters of the Zambezi River rush over Victoria Falls.

Climate, plants and animals

A tropical continent

The **equator** runs right through the middle of Africa. This means that Africa has a lot of hot, tropical areas, more than any other continent. The hottest part of Africa is the Sahara Desert, where temperatures can reach close to 60° Celsius (although night-time temperatures in the Sahara can be very cold).

Most areas of Africa either get huge amounts of rain or very little. The rainforests of central Africa are always wet and rainy. On the other hand, the deserts of northern and southern Africa are usually dry throughout the year. The immense grasslands of Africa can be very wet or very dry, depending on the season. Often a dry season lasts much longer than normal – sometimes for many years – and this makes life very difficult for African farmers.

The African climate has changed a great deal over time. In prehistoric times, the Sahara was much wetter, with lakes, rivers and water-loving animals, such as hippopotamuses and crocodiles. Up to several thousand years ago, there was enough grass for large herds of cattle to graze on parts of the Sahara.

African animals

Animals of northern Africa are similar to the animals of nearby Europe and Asia. These animals include foxes, camels, jerboas and the Barbary ape. The more familiar African animals – such as lions, elephants, giraffes and rhinoceroses – live south of the Sahara desert. Most of the bigger African animals, and those that gather in enormous herds, live in tropical grassland areas, also known as savanna.

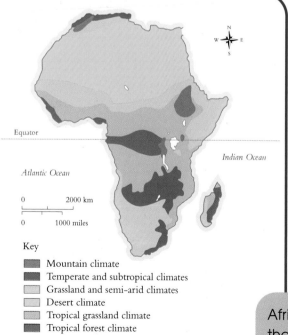

Equator

Indian Ocean

Atlantic Ocean

| 0 | 2000 km |
| 0 | 1000 miles |

Key
- Mountain climate
- Temperate and subtropical climates
- Grassland and semi-arid climates
- Desert climate
- Tropical grassland climate
- Tropical forest climate

Africa has more tropical areas than any other continent.

African plants

African savannas are often scattered with small trees and thorny bushes. Denser vegetation grows in rainforests and swampy areas where mahogany, palms, mangroves and many kinds of fruit trees grow. Dense vegetation can also grow on mountain slopes, including cedar, bamboo, ferns and mosses.

Threats to wildlife

African plants and animals were once more abundant than they are today. Many kinds of wildlife are threatened from too much hunting or the destruction of their natural **habitat**. Some African countries have set aside large reserves or national parks where the animals are protected. Even so, rangers have to patrol these parks to protect the animals from **poachers**.

Grasslands

- lion
- cheetah
- leopard
- hyena
- jackal
- elephant
- rhinoceros
- impala
- wildebeest
- dik-dik
- giraffe
- zebra
- aardvark
- warthog
- baboon
- rock hyrax
- ostrich
- vulture
- sand fox
- springbok
- African wild ass
- Addax antelope
- oryx
- sand rat
- tortoise
- scorpion
- puff-adder viper
- armadillo lizard
- desert locust

Lakes, rivers and swamps

- hippopotamus
- crocodile
- flamingo
- pelican
- stork

Deserts

- camel (domesticated)
- fennec

Tropical forests and woodlands

- chimpanzee
- gorilla
- colobus monkey
- mangabey
- mandrill
- bush baby
- potto
- okapi
- bushbuck
- giant forest hog
- Congo peacock
- hornbill
- grey parrot
- bird snake
- chameleon

Herds of animals live in Africa's tropical grassland areas.

AFRICA

Some of the greatest kingdoms of the ancient world started in Africa. One of the most powerful was Egypt, which began in the Nile Valley more than 5000 years ago. Egypt is still an important country, even though it has been conquered many times by other **empires**, including the Greek, Roman, Arab and Turkish. Other early African empires and kingdoms include those of the Ethiopians, Sudanese, Kushites and Zulus.

Struggle for independence

Europeans began invading Africa more than 2000 years ago. Europeans were interested in trading goods, establishing colonies, mining gold and capturing slaves. Less than a century ago, most of Africa was ruled by European countries, including England, France, Portugal and Belgium. After a period of protest and conflict during the 1900s, the African countries finally became independent. Even so, millions of Africans still speak a European language.

Population groups

For thousands of years, Africans have been travelling across the Sahara Desert. Such a journey can be long and difficult, and many population groups of Africa are still divided by this desert. Most people who live around the north of the Sahara are Arabs, Tuaregs or Berbers. Their way of life is similar to the Arabs of nearby Asia. Most people who live to the south of the Sahara are Black Africans such as Pygmies, Zulus or Bushmen. There are more than 800 of these Black cultural groups, each with its own different language and religion.

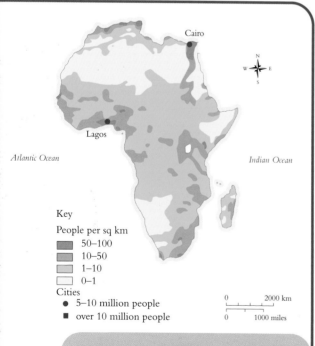

Cairo

N
W   E
S

Lagos

Atlantic Ocean

Indian Ocean

Key

People per sq km
- 50–100
- 10–50
- 1–10
- 0–1

Cities
- ● 5–10 million people
- ■ over 10 million people

0   2000 km
0   1000 miles

Most parts of Africa are thinly populated. Despite Africa's high birthrate, many people die from disease, starvation and warfare.

Despite these differences, most Africans – north and south of the Sahara – have certain things in common. African families are larger than the typical European family, and sometimes husbands have two or more wives. Most Africans live in country areas and grow crops or look after animals. Most of these animals and crops are not African in origin. For example, corn and **cassava** are American crops that were brought to Africa more than a century ago to feed slaves who were waiting to be shipped overseas. Farming in Africa can be difficult, with problems caused by droughts, floods, poor soil, animal disease and insect pests.

- **Islam** and **Christianity** are the two most common religions of Africa.
- Some languages of southern Africa make a clicking sound for certain words. These languages are known as click languages.
- Africa is a big producer of farm and mineral products, but not so much of manufactured products. South Africa is one of the few African countries with significant manufacturing industries, such as iron and steel, automobiles, chemicals, clothing and processed foods.
- Only one in every 25 Africans owns a television set.

Africans can belong to Arab, European, Asian or Black African cultures.

GLOSSARY

barren wasteland, not capable of producing crops

Buddhism a religion based on the teachings of Buddha; followers are called Buddhists

cassava a tropical plant with thick, edible roots

Christianity the Christian religion, based on the teachings of Jesus; followers are called Christians

colonised to have settled in a region, controlling the land and its people

conifers non-flowering trees or shrubs that bear cones. The leaves can have a needle, oval, scale or barbed shape.

deciduous trees trees that shed their leaves during a certain time of the year, such as autumn

domesticated tamed for human use, such as a cow, sheep or dog

empire a group of territories or peoples controlled by one government

equator an imaginary line around the middle of the Earth's surface

fertile rich in nutrients

geographers people who study geography, the study of the Earth's surface

habitats the natural environment of an animal or plant

Hinduism a religion based on ancient beliefs of India; followers are called Hindus

ice age a time when parts of the Earth became colder and were covered by glaciers. There have been many ice ages in ancient history.

Islam the Muslim religion, based on the teachings of the prophet Mohammed; followers are called Muslims

Judaism the Jewish religion, based on the Torah (the Old Testament of the Bible); followers are called Jews

landmass a large area of land, such as a continent

mineral wealth abundance of minerals such as gold, iron and coal

nomadic moving from place to place to find water, food or grass

palm oil butter-like fat obtained from the fruit of palm oil trees. Palm oil is used for a variety of products, including margarine, soap and candles.

peninsulas areas of land almost surrounded by water

poachers people who hunt or trap wild animals illegally

sorghum a tall cereal plant used for feeding livestock or for making products like molasses and syrup

standard of living the level of goods and income enjoyed by a society

temperate moderate; not permanently hot or cold. Temperate climates are those with temperate characteristics, such as a Mediterranean or a cool temperate climate.

tropical of the tropics, the warm regions around the equator

tundra cold, treeless plains around the Arctic region

FURTHER INFORMATION

Websites

About Geography **http://geography.about.com**
Includes sites for world atlas and maps, glossary, quizzes and homework help.

National Geographic **www.nationalgeographic.com**
Includes sites for travel, maps, nature, history and culture.

Books

Lands and Peoples. Grolier Incorporated, Danbury, 1995.

Petersen, D. *True Books* series (*Europe, Asia* and *Africa*). Children's Press, New York, 1998.

The Usborne-Internet-Linked Encyclopedia of World Geography. Usborne Publishing Ltd, London, 2001.

World Explorer series. Prentice Hall, Needham, 1998.

INDEX